GOOGLE CLASSROOM FOR TEACHERS

THE EASY AND EFFECTIVE GUIDE TO MASTER YOUR ONLINE CLASSROOM

EMILY ROSE JOHNSON

or monetary loss due to the information herein, either directly or indirectly.

Table of Contents

Introduction

Google describes Google Classroom as "mission control for your own classroom," and this could be the simplest way to consider doing it. In other words, it is a platform that joins together the G-Bundle tools for both pupils and teachers of Google. Additionally, it serves as a tool in which course materials can be kept by educators and discuss them with pupils— most of the paperless work. From that point, you can select and choose its integration with the favorite tools of Google, and this flexibility, is probably what makes Google Classroom the best among the very EdTech tools that are widely used now.

More than just making the workloads easy, Google Classroom helps educators, teachers, and facilitators to motivate their students. The possibilities are endless as to how they can utilize the many features of Google Classroom for the betterment of the students.

Flipped Classroom

Flipped classroom refers to a type of learning or an instructional strategy that reverses the physical or traditional learning environment by moving activities, resources, and instructional content online.

Students now have access to learning materials; even they are outside the classroom, such as watching instructional videos and reading lectures or articles online. If they can do this at home while class time will be allocated only for discussions, problem-solving, question and answer portion, and debates.

Google Classroom is said to be an efficient tool to flip an entire class. You see, in a flipped classroom, learning could be personalized to cater to every student's learning pace and ability. It is as if giving them the ownership of their own learning process and development, and Google Classroom helps them to achieve such.

The Classroom is a safe venue for discussions while students can review the contents and materials. Teachers, on the other hand, can immediately clarify misconceptions or further explain the topics to students.

Productivity

Again, Google Classroom is a one-stop teacher shop when it comes to class activities. They are able to streamline the digital workflow, push out announcements, disseminate assignments, and engage students to interact during class. Both students and teachers can gain benefit from the workflow.

They can use their own device and gain access to student's work anywhere as long as they have an internet connection.

Collaboration

To date, 30 million faculty, staff, and students are using Google Apps for Education. The free suite for schools includes other educational platforms and tools from Google. The Chromebooks are being used by thousands of students and teachers and use Google apps for school-related matters.

In Classroom, teachers are able to co-teach a class, and students can interact with the teachers and other students. Everything becomes possible with Google Classroom and one can learn even outside the confines of four walls.

More Functions for Teachers

- They can align their curriculum with other educators, given that they have the same domain.

- Share data and materials with a professional learning community.

- Gather weekly or annual feedback from students through Google Forms.

- Share writing samples, anonymously in the classroom.

- Discuss assignment criteria and other requirements.

- Develop mobile learning experiences for students.

- Post announcements for parents.

- Come up with a list of the approved resources that the students can use.

- Divide the resources according to criteria such as student's level, the difficulty of comprehension, groupings, etc.

- Encourage interaction among students, though, commenting each other's posts or assignments. Promote interaction among students, schools, and faculties.

- Manage the setting for viewing, editing, copying and downloading of files to protect the classroom file.

Chapter 1: Why Is Google Classroom a Great Tool for Everybody?

So what is so great about Google Classroom for both teachers and students? Well, read on to find out. Google Classroom is great for both educators and for students, and it ultimately does make it easier for teachers to do their job. Some teachers may be against technological changes, but there are many benefits to this.

Better Accessibility

Google Classroom can be accessed from any device that uses Google Chrome, regardless of platform. This means, you can work on your assignments on an iPad, or even on a mobile phone, and they're uploaded to Google drive and the classroom folder, meaning they can be used wherever, whenever, and students never have to worry about losing their assignments anymore, that's for sure!

Saves Paper!

Google Classroom is completely paperless, so you won't have to worry about printing thirty-plus copies for students that have a knack for losing their papers, nor do you have to worry about students misplacing paper well, it's all online. All of the assignments are uploaded and saved to the drive, which means that students can complete the assignments there, send it, and it's completely saved, even if they don't, it's there, so you will never have to worry about students using the "my computer crashed" excuse for the third time.

Exposes both Teachers and Students to Online Learning

Since it's all online, Google Classroom allows students to work in an online environment, which is something that students will soon learn about the moment they go to college. If you want a master's degree in education, you need to actually do some of your work online. The same goes for many majors, but many students don't know how to navigate an online class. Well, Google Classroom is a great way to actually understand how to work in an online environment, and by being exposed to it early on, it allows for them to not be as shell-shocked when they finally make their way to college and realize that they'll have a lot of classes similar to this in the future.

Super easy to Get Materials

It's also super easy to access the materials, but this is good because no matter where they end up, they'll get them. Students that are absent can get the classroom materials from home if needed by simply logging in and getting the assignments by clicking. The days of having to deal with students have to chase after you just to get assignments are gone.

All Work is there

One thing that's super annoying and frustrating for teachers is the fact that some students have a knack for losing work. Well, Google Classroom nips that in the bud. How? Well, it takes out that external document, and instead, everyone works in Google drive. Google Drive saves everything immediately, regardless of if you make one change to add a word, or if you work on the assignment for hours on end. It's super nice, and it saves you a lot of headaches. It's all there, and students never have to worry about "accidentally" losing work.

Creates Collaborative Learning

Because everything is digital, you can share content with peers in one singular document that can be edited together, and then share another version for the students without the editing to this. If you want to, you can create assignment worksheets that are different for teachers and students, and from there, drive together with a question and answer system, and even create deeper discussions. It allows teachers to really engage with students. With the way technology is bringing everyone together, it's no wonder why teachers want to integrate this further and further into the classroom.

Instant Feedback and Analysis

Gone are the days of having to wait for whether or not you did well on a quiz, or if you will get enough answers. Teachers don't have to sit around and meticulously spend a ton of time grading assignments. Instead, you can deliver quizzes that have automatic answers, or even give a detailed report on what teachers can do better. You can help those who answered questions incorrectly add more to this, which is super nice, and it is super easy to integrate into the system. Students will get their answers faster, and teachers can grade everything in a more detailed way.

Saves you a Ton of Time

For students, this saves a lot of their time trying to save various documents, hoping that it gets to their drive, or even just working on paper and awkwardly turning it in. It also saves them time on answering questions, because let's be honest, a day could go by, and they may not get the answer right away. By utilizing Google Classroom, you can save yourself. A boatload of time, and ultimately participate way more in this as well.

Communication Success

This ties into the previous point, but Google Classroom saves you a ton of time when it comes to communicating. If a student has a question, they can send an e-mail, comment on an assignment stream, send comments privately, or even provide feedback on something. Teachers can do the same, and the teachers can as well send specific e-mails to communicate with students that have a specific issue, or who need a lot more help. That way, they won't fall behind. It is making a difference in terms of how students handle the workload, and teachers can also follow the different standards, and in truth, it makes it so much easier for everyone.

Students Take Ownership

One thing that teachers try to help students get better at is trying to stay more engaged in their studies. Well, Google Classroom can help with this. It is not just students reading and commenting on answers that the other students may have: it is also being in charge of their homework. Students can teach a subject they're having trouble with a little bit better if they are struggling with it, and in turn, if they want to utilize additional resources on their won, they can. The best part of Google Classroom is that students can take charge of their learning environment, and in turn, create the best learning experience that they can.

In-Depth Data Analysis Good Security

If you want to see whether or not students understand, and any areas they may be stumbling on, this is how.

You can even take the grades and export them from Google sheets, or just keep everything there. If you want to analyze and sort them as well, in order to see how students are faring and where you need to focus, you can use this as a super helpful resource tool.

Lots of times, you can see trends in grades, and if you notice there is something wrong with a student's learning, you can take the information that's there, and from there, use this to help students get a better idea of what is going on.

Teachers can get more involved with the use of Google Classroom, and they can see just where their students need some help, and any other resources that can assist them as well to be successful.

Good Security

Security is actually very strong on this. If you have an IT team, they can control the passwords, so if a student does forget, they can fix it quickly. With the API that is there, everything is synced up, so the teachers can have everything put together. It also got high-level security, which means that you won't have to worry about any breaches and the like, for it's also quite easy to work with.

See that Real-Time Progress

Are you sick of trying to have to walk around and see whether students are working on this, or maybe you want to help students if they are going in the wrong direction? Well, now you can with this. With the Google Classroom system, you can press Student Work, and you can look at the thumbnail of every single student in order to see their progress in real-time, so you can track and see if there are any problems if you are looking to change this. You can also use the revision history feature to look at changes that have happened, allowing you to see what worked, or what didn't work, and how you can fix that.

Chapter 2: Getting Started, Basics of Google Classroom

Getting Started

It is only going to take a few minutes to create a new class or post resources or even set permissions for your students. After you have done this, you are going to be able to invite students directly to the class or by sending them a code.

Creating classes

1. On a computer, you are going to go to www.classroom.google.com.

2. Select the plus sign then click on "create class" button.

3. You will then enter the name of the class.

4. Enter in text like grade level and what time the class is.

5. Also put a subject line in.

6. Select "create."

Your class is going to automatically be given a code that is going to be used to invite students. You have the option of changing the themes and putting a photo for the class. If you should not need the class, anymore you can archive it.

Accepting provisioned classes

Whoever manages the classroom is going to be able to create classes for their teachers as well as adding students to them. Any classes that are made by the administrator are going to be placed in a provisioned state. As the teacher, you will need to sign in and accept the invitation to the class before it is visible to students:

1. Go to www.classroom.google.com.

2. Move to the class's card and click "accept."

3. Ensure that the number of students in the class is accurate before you click on "accept."

Changing the theme

Once you have created the class, you have the option of changing the image and colors of the class. Only teachers have the ability to change the theme:

1. Sign into classroom.Google.com.

2. Move to the bottom of the class image and click on the "select theme" button.

3. Pick one of the following options:

    a. Pick a pattern.

    b. Choose an image from the gallery.

Uploading your own image

1. Open your class and pick "upload photo."

2. Pick one of these options:

    a. Move a picture over to the middle of the screen.

    b. Select a photo from your computer.

Editing class information

1. Enter classroom.Google.com into your URL.

2. Move to the class card and select the three little dots. A menu will pop up, which will give you the option of editing the class.

3. Enter the new information and hit save.

Displaying a profile picture

You have the ability to place a photo next to the name of your class. Automatically your classroom is going to use your Google account photo so you will want to make sure that you are using an appropriate picture.

Problems creating classes

In the event that you are using a G-Suite Education account and find that you are unable to add classes, then the administrator of the suite is going to need to verify that you are a teacher in their domain. So, make sure that you are contacting your administrator for any help that you may need.

Note: should you be using a personal Google account, then you are going to be limited on how many classes you are going to be able to create.

Adding a class to a resource page

Once a class has been created, you are going to have the ability to add information and resources to your class in the about page. You are going to be able to post materials and instructions so that they can know how you grade, what to expect throughout the year, so on and so forth. This information can be added or removed at any point in time.

Adding class information

1. Go to the website www.classroom.google.com.

2. Move to the about section. The name of the class is going to automatically be entered there.

3. You can add a description or a location for the class. But, if you leave these fields blank, they are not going to appear in what the students see for your class.

4. Save.

Resource materials

1. Under the class information section, you will see a button that says add class materials and a title can be entered there.

2. You will have the option of adding in multiple resources less than one title or adding them separately under specific names.

   a. If you need to attach a file, click on the appropriate icon.

   b. Find the item that you want to attach and click "Add" if you decide that you do not need that item anymore, just click on "Remove."

   c. Post.

Your e-mail address and a link to the folder, where the attachment is located will be automatically included with every item that is added to the resource page. This cannot be changed.

Editing your about page

1. Go to the classroom web page.

2. Move to the about section.

3. Click on the three dots and select the edit button.

4. Make any changes that you see fit and then save them.

Joining classes by invitation

You can not only create your own class, but you can be invited to classes so that you can become a co-teacher in a class. Co-teachers are going to have the option of performing all of the teacher tasks once they have joined that class.

Accepting an invitation

1. Go to the classroom web page.

2. Accept the invitation or decline it if you do not want to be a co-teacher.

3. You can also select the invitation through the e-mail that you get.

Note: when a student declines the invitation to become a co-teacher, they are not going to be removed from the class.

Permissions for Co-teachers

These permissions are going to need to be made aware of by all of the teachers in a class.

- Only the main teacher has the ability to delete the class.

- Co-teachers who join a class can access the Google Drive folder.

- Primary teachers cannot withdraw or be removed from their own class.

- Teachers cannot be muted.

- The primary teacher is the owner of the Google Drive folder.

Class size

G-Suite accounts

If you are using a G-Suite account, then you are going to be able to have up to twenty teachers and a thousand members of both teachers and students.

Note: Classrooms are going to use groups for the students and teachers that are using the education suite accounts. Every person is only going to be allowed in a certain number of groups.

Personal accounts

When using a personal account, there are going to be other limits put on activities such as creating or inviting people.

Basics of Google Classroom

The great thing about Google Classroom is that it ties together many of the other products from Google to provide a paperless system for educational institutions to use. You will be able to use Google Drive to create and distribute assignments, and Gmail is good for sending information to the students. Google Calendar helps the students know when different assignments are due to and even when other important events, such as tests, will occur. Get class can also use Google Docs to submit assignments, and the teacher can then view and grade the homework.

All of these works together to make things easier for students and teachers, communication is done just through regular e-mails, and it takes just a few seconds for the teacher to create assignments and for students to submit their work. Also, Google Classroom does not use ads in the program, so no one has to worry about this interfering with the work or about Google collecting private information.

Assignments

Google Drive is going to be the main point of contact for assignments with Google Classroom. Teachers can either look at documents the students have uploaded, and grade from there, or they can upload a template that each student can change and resubmit as their own. This can be helpful if the teacher needs a worksheet or discussion questions answered for homework. Also, if the student needs to attach supporting documents, this can easily be done in Google Drive as well.

Grading

Teachers can choose the way that they would like to grade on this platform. One option is just to have the students submit the work, and teachers can choose to grade by marking answers correct or not before sending the information back. On other assignments, such as projects that will take some time or for essays, the teacher can track progress, make edits and even grade with notes and send it back for revisions.

There are several applications that can assist with this grading option as well. Flubaroo is perfect if you have worksheets or multiple-choice tests that simply need to be graded. This application can take the assignment, grade it automatically, and then send the grade to the students, so they get feedback right away, even when the teacher is busy.

Communication

Most of the communication can be done through Gmail. Teachers can send announcements, homework assignments and other information to students and they can send questions and information back to the teacher when it is most convenient for them. Gmail is easy to use, and it only takes a few minutes for students to create their accounts if they don't already have one.

In addition to using Gmail, Google Drive, and YouTube can be used for communications. Teachers can post to Google Drive the new assignments and announcements the students need. YouTube can be great for sending videos and other media when it pertains to the classroom.

Time-cost

First, cost. This platform is free to use, both for the teacher and the students. The teacher simply needs to create their classroom and then send the code to their students. This allows the students to get into the classroom, access any announcements and assignments, and even to ask their questions. The classroom is secure, so only those invited can see what is inside, and since Google doesn't allow advertisements, parents know that it is safe.

Next, the amount of time the teachers can save using this platform is immense. They can add on applications that grade worksheets and homework automatically for them. They won't have to waste time at the copy machine or handing out papers to all the students. They can spend their class time teaching and save the announcements and homework assignments for later.

Mobile Version

Google has also made a mobile version of Classroom that allows for even more features including the ability to snap photos and add them to assignments, share other apps including web pages, PDF's, and images, and the ability to get their homework assignments even when they aren't around an internet connection. This is available for both Android and iPhone products, making it easier for everyone to use.

Google Classroom is designed to make education easier. Teachers can spend more time interacting with their students and less time worrying about all the paperwork while students can easily get to their important announcements and upload homework assignments on their time. With the ability to work on many of the popular Google apps, this is one of the best free platforms to help with education.

Chapter 3: Setting up and Manage the Classroom

Classes are fun to create, and we will go over in this chapter how you create a class, organize and manage the class, and how you can remove classes once they are done. Classes are the most important aspect of this since it's where everyone will be, and if you know how to put all of this together, you'll be well on your way to a successful result with Google Classroom.

How to Set-up a Class

Now, once you've logged in and everything, it's time to create a class. When you first do log in, you get the option of either student or teacher. Always make sure that you indicate that you are a teacher, and if you mess up, you need to contact the administrator to reset this. It's super important, because students are limited in their options compared to teachers, and it can be quite frustrating. Now, if you're a student, you simply press when you get the plus button to join a class. For teachers, it's creating a class.

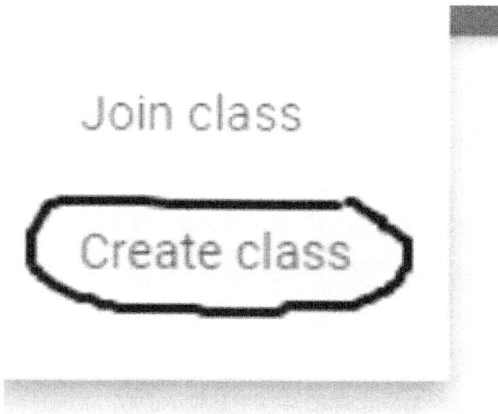

Now, if you've already got classes, chances are you'll see some other names there. They'll be displayed on the screen itself, but every time you press the plus button, you'll then be able to add more to this.

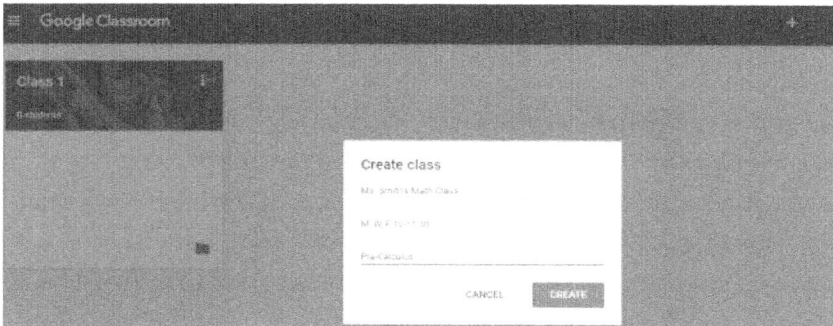

Next, you're given a class dialogue boss. You'll then type in the name and the section of this. You'll be able to immediately create the class from here.

But, if you want to add more to it, you can go to the about tab, choose the title of the course, along with the description of this, the location of this, and even add materials here. You do need to have a name for the class since this is how students will find it when they open it up. If you have classes with multiple names on it, you'll definitely want to specify, either via time or day, especially if you've got a lot of sections. The section field is how you do this, and you can create a subject as well, based on the list of subjects they provide for you.

Some teachers like to make these very descriptive, and you should ideally add as much information as you feel that you need for this. But remember that you make sure that it isn't some wall of text that students will read and get confused. As a teacher, you should make sure that you do this in a way where students will get the information easily, and that they'll be able to delineate each class. It's also important to make it easy for your own benefit.

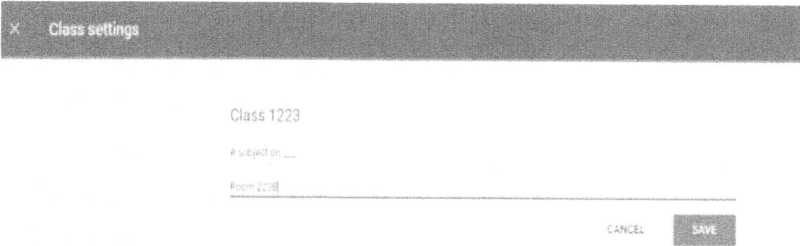

How to Manage a Class

The first thing that you can do when you change the class and managing it is giving it a theme. One thing that you'll notice is that you don't have students in there once it's created, so you can have a bit of fun with this. A way you can do it is on the right side near the header of the general class, and is you need to change the class theme. You can use the themes that are there to be offered. Some photos of classes themselves are good options, and you can use different templates for each one so you know what class you're using because themes can sometimes be a bit complicated.

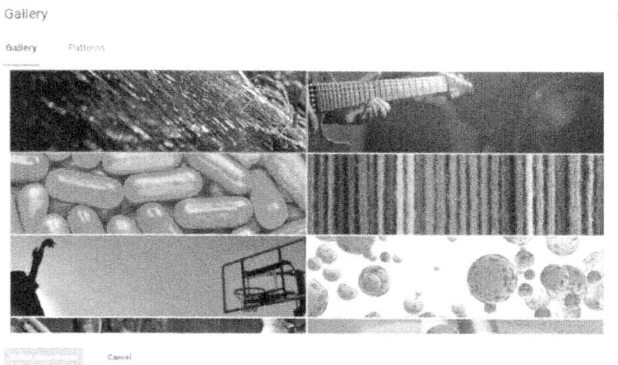

How to Remove, Delete, and View a Class

When using Google Classroom, sometimes you'll want to delete a class when it's the end of the semester, and you can always restore it if you need it. You can also delete it if you never want to see the class again, or have no use for it because you've got the assignments already. Now, if you don't achieve these, they stick around, so make sure you do it.

Now archived classes essentially mean that they're in an area where you have the materials, the work students have, and the posts. You can view it, but you can't actually use it and it is good if a student wants the materials.

Archiving classes is simple to do. You choose the class; see the three dots, press it and then, it is archived.

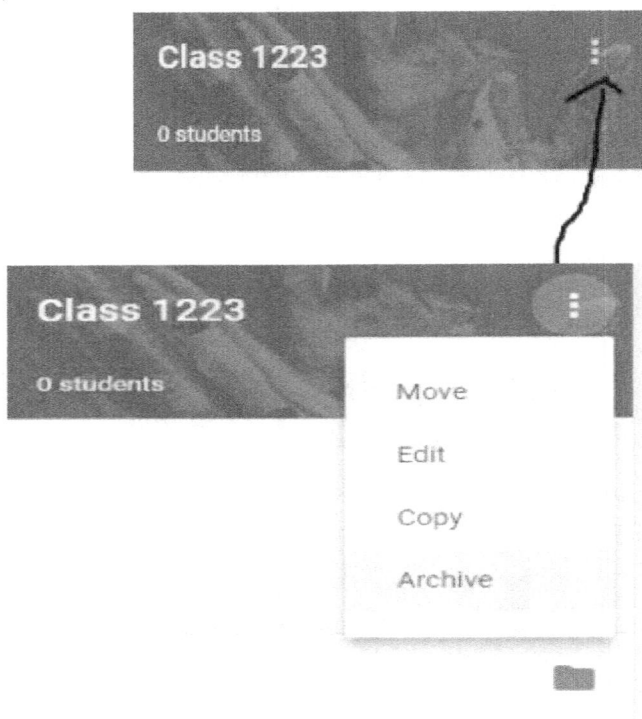

Now to view an archived class after it's been archived, you press the three-line menu, go down to the tab that says achieve classes, and then choose the class you want to see.

To delete a class, though, you essentially have to do the same thing. Remember that you need to archive the class before you can delete it, scroll all the way down, click on archive classes, and from there, once you have the classes, press the three dots option, and then choose to delete this. From there, you'll have the class fully removed. Remember though, you can't undo this once you've done this, and if you do choose to delete a class, you don't have access to the comments or the posts, but if you have any files that are in the drive, you can always access those, since you have those in the class files themselves.

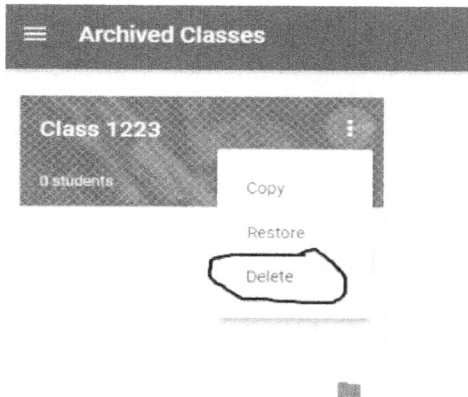

Other Tips and Tricks for class Management

There are a few class management things that you can implement, and some tips and tricks that go into Google Classroom. The first thing that happens is when you get to the classes tab on there, and you want to drag and move the classes around, you could do so. This is a good way to change the order of this, and it's quite easy to do.

Another important thing to remember too is that you have the classroom function. It's quite nice, and if you want to change the calendar or view it, you essentially can press the icon with the calendar that's on there, and you can even check it out to see what's coming up for every single class, because some classes may do certain things at different times of the semester.

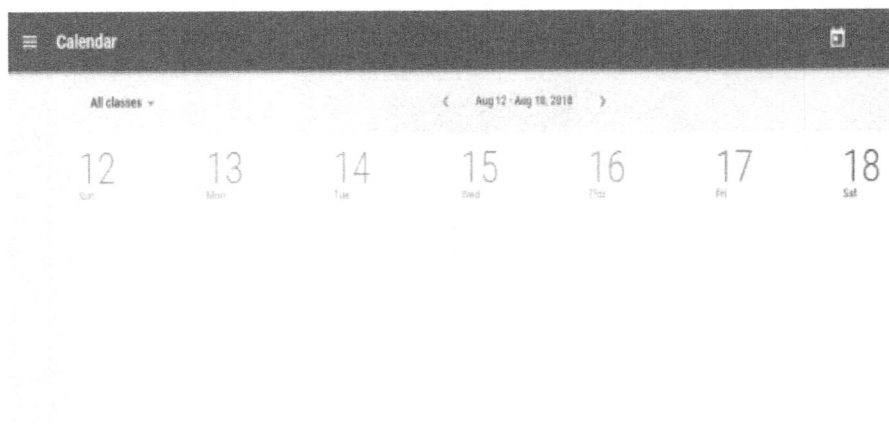

Finally, you can always adjust the settings at any point. This is done with the gear that you see on the home screen. Here, you can change the name of the class, especially if it's confusing, show the class code if you need it, and also decide on the stream showcase whether or not you want items to be deleted or displayed. There are other features there too, and it's all right there waiting for you to be used.

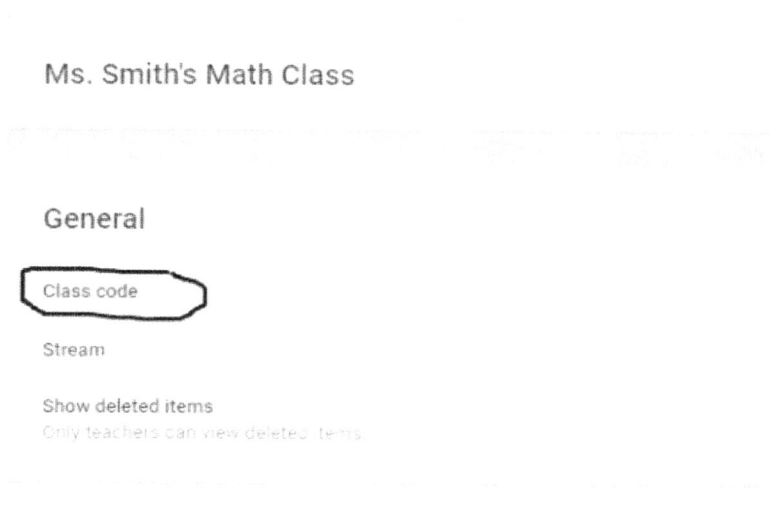

Ms. Smith's Math Class

General

Class code

Stream

Show deleted items
Only teachers can view deleted items

When it comes to Google Classroom, knowing how to create the classes is a big part of it. If you have classes that you want to add, or you want to get started with Google Classroom, this is the way to go, and it's the surefire way to success with this.

Chapter 4: How to Set Due Dates, Manage Homework and Assignments

Overview

Assignments are a useful tool on Google Classroom for delivering, tracking, and also grading student submissions. Even submissions that are non-electronic can also be tracked using the Assignments tool.

Add an Assignment

Creating an Assignment

- Open www.classroom.google.com.

- At the top, click on "Class" and open "Classwork."

- Also, click on "Create" and click on "Assignment."

- Input the title and necessary instructions.

Posting Assignment

A. To one or more classes:

- Just below for, click the drawdown on "Class."

- Choose the Class you want to include.

B. To individual students:

- Select a class and click the drawdown on "All Student."

- Uncheck "All Students."

- Then select the particular student(s).

Inputting grade category

- Click the drawdown on "Grade Category."

- Select "Category."

- Edit the following (Optional):

- Click "Grades" to edit the grades page.

- Click "Instructions" to compose the Assignment.

- Click "Classwork" to create a homework, quiz, and test.

Change the point value

- Click the drawdown below points.

- Create a new point value or click "ungraded."

Edit due date or Time

- Click on the drawdown below "Due."

- Click on the dropdown on "No due date."

- Fix date on the Calendar.

- Create due Time by clicking Time, input a time adding AM or PM.

Add a topic

- Click on the drawdown below Topic.

- Click on "Create Topic" and input the topic name.

- Click on an existing topic to select it.

Insert Attachments

File

- Click on "Attach."

- Search for the file and select it.

- Click "Upload."

Drive

- Click on "Drive."

- Search for the item and click it.

- Click "Add."

YouTube

- Click on YouTube.

- Type in the keyword on the search bar and click search.

- Select the video.

- Click "Add."

For video link URL

- Click on YouTube and select URL.

- Input the URL and Add.

Link

- Click on Link.

- Select the URL.

- Click on "Add link."

You can delete an attachment

- Click removes or the cross sign beside it.

You can also determine the number of students that interacts with the Attachment:

- Click on the drawdown besides the "Attachment."

- Select the required option:

- Students can View File – This implies that students are allowed to read the data but cannot edit it.

- Students can edit the file – This means students can write and share the same data.

- Make a personal copy of each student – This means students can have their transcript with their name on the file and can still have access to it even when turned in until the teacher return it to them.

Note: If you encounter an issue like, no permission to attach a file, click on copy. This will make Classroom make a copy, which is attached to the Assignment and saved to the class Drive folder.

Add a Rubric

You must have titled the Assignment before you create a rubric.

- Click the "Add" sign beside Rubric.

- Click on "Create rubric."

- Turn off scoring by clicking the switch to off, besides the Use scoring.

- Using scoring is optional, click "Ascending or Descending" beside the Sort the order of points.

Note: using scoring, gives you the room to add a performance level in any with the levels arranged by point value automatically.

- You can input Criterion like Teamwork, Grammar, or Citations. Click the criterion title.

- Add Criterion description (Optional.) Click the Criterion description and input the description.

Note: You can add multiple performance level and Criterion.

- Input points by entering the number of points allotted.

Note: The total rubric score auto-updates as points are added.

- Add A level title, input titles to distinguish performance level, e.g., Full Mastery, Excellent, Level A.

- Add a Description, input expectations for each performance level.

- Rearrange Criterion by clicking "More" and select "Up or Down."

- Click "Save" on the right corner to save Rubric.

Reuse Rubric

- Click on the "Add" sign beside "Rubric."

- Click "Reuse Rubric."

- Enter "Select Rubric" and click on the title. You can select Rubric from a different class by entering the class name OR by clicking the drawdown and select the Class.

- View or Edit rubric, click on "preview," click on "Select and Edit" to edit, save changes when it's done. Go back and click "Select to view."

View rubric assignments

- Click on "Rubric."

- Click the arrow up down icon for Expand criteria.

- Click the arrow down up icon for Collapse criteria.

The grading rubric can be done from the Student work page or the grading tool.

Sharing a Rubric

This is possible through export. The teacher creates the Rubric exports, and these are saved to a class Drive called Rubric Exports. This folder can be shared with other teachers and imported into their Assignment.

The imported Rubric can be edited by the teacher in their Assignment, and this editing should not be carried out in the Rubric Exports folder.

Export

- Click on "Rubric."

- Click "More" on the top-right corner and enter "Export to Sheets."

- Return to Classwork page by clicking close (cross sign) at the top-left corner.

- At the top of the Classwork page, click on Drive folder and enter My Drive.

- Select an option, to share one rubric, right-click the "Rubric." To share a rubric folder, right-click on the folder.

- After right-clicking, click on Share and input the e-mail you are sharing to.

- Then click "Send."

Import

- Click on the "Add" sign beside "Rubric" and enter "Import from Sheets."

- Click on the particular "Rubric" you want and click on "Add."

- Edit the Rubric (Optional.)

- Click on "Save."

Editing Rubric Assignment

- Click on the "Rubric."

- Click on "More" at the top-right corner and enter "Edit."

- Click "Save" after making changes.

Deleting Rubric Assignment

- Click on "Rubric."

- Click on "More" at the top-right corner and enter "Delete."

- Click "Delete" to confirm.

Posting, Scheduling, or Saving Draft Assignment

Post

- Open Classwork and click on Assignment.

- Click on the drawdown beside Assign, on the top-right corner.

- Click on Assign to post the "Assignment."

Schedule

- Click on the drawdown beside "Assign," on the top-right corner

- Enter "Schedule."

- Input and the date you want the "Assignment" posted.

- Click "Schedule."

Save

- Click on the drawdown beside Assign, on the top-right corner.

- Enter "Save Draft."

- Editing "Assignment:"

- Open "Classwork."

- Click on "More" (three-dot) close to "Assignment:" and enter "Edit."

- Input the changes and save for posted or schedule "Assignment," while Go to Save draft, to save the draft assignment.

Adding Comments to Assignment

- Open "Classwork."

- Click "Assignment" and Enter "View Assignment."

- Click on "Instructions at the top."

- Click on "Add Class Comment."

- Input your comment and Post.

To Reuse Announcement and Assignment

Announcement

- Open the Class.

- Select "Stream."

- Slide into the Share something with your class box and click on a square clockwise up and down arrow or "Reuse" post.

Assignment

- Open "Classwork" and click on "Create."

- Click on a square clockwise up and down arrow or "Reuse" post.

- Select the "Class and Post" you want to reuse.

- Then click on "Reuse."

Delete an Assignment

- Open "Classwork."

- Click on More (three-dot) close to "Assignment."

- Click on "Delete" and confirm it.

Creating a Quiz Assignment

- Open "Classwork" and click on "Create."

- Click "Quiz Assignment."

- Input the title and instructions.

- You can switch on Locked mode on Chromebooks to ensure student can't view other pages when taking the quiz.

- You can switch on "Grade Importing" to import grades.

Response and Return of Grades

Response

- Open "Classwork."

- Click on "Quiz Assignment" and free "Quiz Attachment."

- Click on "Edit" and input "Response."

Return

- Open "Classwork."

- Click on "Quiz Assignment."

- Pick the student and click on "Return."

- Confirm "Return."

Chapter 5: How to Invite Students and Add Co-Teachers to Classes

The first step that you will need to work on is adding in a class. You will need to do the following steps for each of the classes that you are going to teach for the year, but since they are pretty simple to set up, you won't have a lot of work to do. To add one of your first classes in Google Classroom, you would use the following steps if working inside of a web browser:

- Go to www.classroom.google.com and then sign in with your credentials.

- Click on the (+) sign, and then on "Create Class."

- Look around to see the first empty text box, and then place it in the name that you would like to name the class.

- Under the name of the class, you will want to add a short description. There should be a second text box for you to be able to do this. You can also add in the section, the grade level, or the class time to make it easier to find the class.

- When all of this is set up, you will just need to click on the create button to get the class started.

The steps above are all about working on a web browser on your personal computer. If you would like to use your iOS device to set up the class, you would use the following steps.

- Go to your classroom.google.com account, and then click on the icon that kind of looks like a person.

- From here, you can click on, or use your fingers, the (+) sign and then click on Create Class.

- From here, you will need to add in the information for the class that you are working on. You can enter the name of the class as well as a small description of the class in your second box.

- When all of the right information is inside of the boxes, you can click on "Create" and your class is ready.

You can also choose to set up one of these classrooms with the help of your Android device. Some of the steps that you can take to use your Android device include:

- Go to the classroom.google.com and use your credentials to sign in.

- Look for the icon that looks like a person and click on that to start.

- Touch on the (+) sign and then push "Create Class."

- Enter the name of the class, as well as the description and the other information that you would like to use in the second box.

- When all of this is in the right place, you can click on create, and then your class is all ready to go.

Adding-in a Resource Page to the Class

Now that the class is all set up to use, it is time to add some substance to your class, some information that the students will be able to use to get the information that they need. A class resource page is a good place to start because it is the place where you will be able to post some of your instructional materials. This could include some information about grading policies, classroom rules, lessons, and even your syllabus.

This should be a place where you spend some time letting the students know what they can expect when they come onto the page and need to work in your class. Some of the things that you can do to set up the class resource page include:

- Go to your www.classroom.google.com page.

- Choose the class that you want to use to add in a resource page if you have more than one class

- From here you will click on the about button on the top of the page.

- You can then pick out a title and a description for your class from here.

- In-Room Field, add in a location and then leave it blank.

- Click on "Add Materials" to add the different resources that you want to use in the classroom. For example. If the teacher wants to attach a specific file, they will be able to click on the right icon. Then they can locate the item that they want to use and click on Add. If you don't need to add an attachment, just click on "X."

- Once all of the attachments are placed on the resource page, you can click on "Post" and then make sure to save as well.

Add-In Other Teachers

It is also possible to add-in other teachers to the Classroom as well to make learning a bit more enjoyable. If you have another teacher who is working on the same kind of lesson plans, both of you can share the account and share information between your students. This will make it easier for both of you to work together, answer questions, and get more done inside the classroom. Also, if you have a student-teacher or someone else who is working together in the traditional classroom with you, it is a good idea to add them in with teacher privileges in the classroom as well.

When you are ready to add in some more teachers to the Google Classroom, no matter what the reason may be, you will need to go with the following steps to make this happen:

- Go in and sign in to your classroom.google.com account.

- You can then go and pick out the class that you would like to add in another teacher or two to, and then click on the about button that is on the top of the screen.

- Here you should see a button that says "Invite Teacher." Click on that and then put a checkmark in the box that is next to the teachers you would like to invite. They will already need to be in the Google Classroom system for your institution for you to be able to do this.

- If you decide to add-in everyone who is on the list, you can click on "Select All" to make this happen.

- If you notice that one of the teachers that you would like to invite is not on this list, you will just need to click on "My Contacts" and then follow the steps above again.

Adding-in other teachers to your classroom can be a great way to share some of the work, get someone to help you out with a larger class, and even to enhance some of the learning experience for all of the students. There are a few things that you should notice about adding in teachers to your classroom, though. To start, the class can only be deleted by the teacher, who is considered primarily on the account. So, if you set up the class, you will be the only one who can delete the class. The primary teacher can also not be un-enrolled or removed from the class. This is because the primary teacher is going to be the one that owns all of the materials that belong to the class, such as the structures, folders, assignments, and more; this primary teacher were taken off the class, the system would not work properly.

If there is a teacher who is in the class, you are not able to mute them. This means that they will be able to make comments, leave feedback, and more when they are in the classroom. You should make sure that everyone is on the same page for how they are supposed to behave in the class because it will be hard to stop the behavior without removing the teacher completely from the class later.

When your e-mail notifications are on, the primary and the additional teachers are all going to be notified of the comments that the students send in, even if these comments are private. However, you can change this a little bit and ask the students to send an e-mail directly to you, rather than through the messaging system, to make it more private if they would like.

When there are other teachers in the system, they are also able to add in some more materials to the classroom to help with the learning experience. If they do add-in some new materials, all of these materials are going to be found in the primary teacher's folder.

Inviting the Students

Now that you have spent some time getting the Google Classroom all setup, it is time to add in the students. It is not going to be much of a classroom; if all you have, there are some of the teachers. There are a few ways that you can add-in the students who should be in the class, you can choose the one that works for you. Remember that you will need to go through these steps for each of the classes that you set up, so be careful that you are getting the right students into the right classes. Also, before setting this up to you, should remember that all of the classes on Google Classroom will have a maximum of 20 teachers and 1000 students at one time, but this is often going to be way more than you will need for your classes.

As mentioned, there are a few different methods that you can use to get some students into your Classroom. The first method we are going to take a look at is just inviting them to come to joins the class. To do this, you would use the following steps:

Go to your classroom.google.com account.

From here, you will want to work on adding the students to the class that you have chosen. So, go into the chosen class and then click on Students and then invite.

- Tick on the box next to all of the names of the students that you need to add to the class. If all of the students on the list need to be invited, you can click on Select All.

- If you need to see some other lists to get the students that you would like to add in, you will need to click on "My Contacts." You can also click on "Directory" to see some of the other students who are in your domain.

- When your list is all done, you can click on Invite students.

Chapter 6: How to Conduct a Class Discussion

Google Classroom allows you to extend the blended learning experience in a variety of ways. By 2017, teachers can create an excellent number of ways to enhance a student's grasp of school subjects and increase learning capabilities. The possibilities are endless where Google is concerned.

Google's biggest asset is its simplicity and ease of use. Using the various Google applications doesn't require a textbook to learn it. As with Google Classroom, all other apps are simple to set up, quick to learn and save time and energy to get things done and organize your various files and documents. We will share ten best practices for Google Classroom that you can employ to fully make use and take advantage of this pioneering online education tool.

1. Reduce the carbon footprints of your class

The idea of Google Classroom is to make things easier for teachers and students alike when learning things. It takes the conventional classroom and places it on the online sphere and enables students and educators to create spreadsheets and presentations, online documents, and makes sharing and communicating easier. Creating and sharing things digitally eliminates the need for printing. Schools use a lot of papers, but utilizing Classroom enables you to remove the necessity of paper for simple things. Do you have an assignment? Save some trees, time, and money by creating them in the Classroom and distributing it to your students in your Classroom.

2. Distribute and Collect Student's homework easily

The whole point of creating the assignments via Google Classroom is so that you can distribute it and collect the assignments quickly. Yes, you can say that you could get it done via e-mail too. But the Classroom enables all of these things to be done in one place. You'll know who has sent an assignment, who have passed their deadline, and who needs more help with their work. It's all about lessening the hassle in your life.

3. Utilizing the feedback function

With instant access, teachers can clarify doubts, concerns, and misconceptions their students may have by providing feedback as and when students need it. As teachers, you eliminate possible issues that may arise while the students are doing their assignments. This reduces a headache you might have upon receiving the assignments that don't meet the requirements. Assignments that are handed in that have issues can be immediately rectified as well through private one-on-one feedback with the relevant student.

4. Create your personalized learning environment

The main benefit of Google Classroom is the freedom that it gives teachers. Very often, teachers are required to follow the national syllabus forwarded by the Department or Ministry of Education. While this is rightly done for the sake of uniformity and to ensure students across the country have access to the same level of education, utilizing Classroom, on the other hand, gives teachers the freedom to add and create a different environment for learning.

Teachers can focus on using different materials, subjects, and cater to the different levels and needs of the students. If you are using Google Classroom, make sure you use this aspect to your fullest advantage. You would be able to endorse a personalized learning system by giving your students different learning preferences such as choices of submitting answers, various types of online assignments, and using online resources.

The more you use Google Classrooms, the more you will be able to use Classrooms in many different ways than just connecting with your students and creating assignments.

Google Classroom, combined with other Google products such as Google Slides, can deliver powerful interactive user experiences and deliver engaging and valuable content. Teachers looking to create engaging experiences in Google Classroom can use Google Slides and other tools in the Google suite of products to create unique experiences.

Here are some exciting ways that you can use Google Classroom and Google Slides to create an engaging learning experience for your students:

1. Create eBooks via PDF

PDF files are so versatile, and you can open them in any kind of device. Want to distribute information only for read-only purposes? Create a PDF. You can use Google Docs or even Google Slides for this purpose and then save it as a PDF document before sending it out to your classroom.

2. Create a slide deck book

Make your textbooks paperless too, not just assignments. Teachers can derive engaging and interactive content from the web and include it in the slide deck books, upload it to the Google Classroom, and allow your students to access them. Make sure to keep it as read-only.

3. Play Jeopardy

This method has been used in plenty of Google Classrooms, and the idea was created by Eric Curts, who is a Google Certified Innovator. This template can be copied into your own Google Drive so you can customize your question and answers. Scores can be kept on another slide that only you can control.

4. Create Game-Show Style Review Games

Another creative teacher came up with a Google Slide of 'Who Wants to Be a Millionaire?' The template allows you to add in your questions and get students to enter the answers in the text box. Again, you keep the score!

5. Use Animation

Did you know you can create animations in your Google Slide and share them in your Classroom? You can also encourage your students to create an animation to explain their assignments. This is making them push boundaries and think out of the box.

6. Create stories and adventures

Use Google Slides and upload them to Google Classroom to tell a story. Turn a question into something creative and teach your students to create an adventure to describe their decision for the outcome of the character in their story. This method can be a certain path for the students to chose for the character of a story that explains the process of finding a solution.

7. Using Flash Cards

Flashcards are great ways to increase the ability to understand a subject or topic. Do you want to create an interactive session on Google Classroom using flashcards? You can start by utilizing Google Sheets, which gives you a graphic display of words and questions. To reveal the answers, all you need to do is click. Compared to paper flashcards, these digital flashcards allow you to easily change the questions, colors as well as the answers of the cards depending on what you are teaching the class. Digital flashcards are also an interactive presentation method that is guaranteed to engage your Classroom and bring about a new way of teaching using Google Classroom's digital space. Make vocabulary lessons, geography lessons, and even history lessons fun and entertaining with digital flashcards.

8. Host an Online Viewing Party

Get your students to connect to the Classroom at a pre-determined date and time when there is a noteworthy performance, play, or even a movie that is related to the subjects you are teaching in your class. Let them view the video together and also interact with them by adding questions to your Google Classroom and allowing your students to reply to you in real-time. This way, you can assess them on their reflections, level of understanding, and their observations. You can also give your interpretation of the scene and explain it again to students who do not quite understand.

Chapter 7: How to Create and Grade Assignments

Creating an Assignment

Step 1

The Classroom will always be set to Announcement by default. To get started, click "Assignment" on your page.

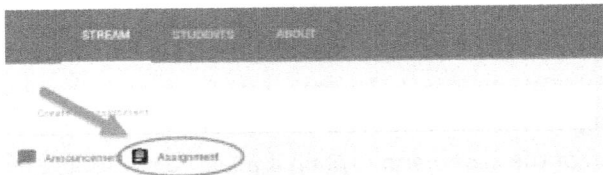

Step 2

Enter the name and description of your task.

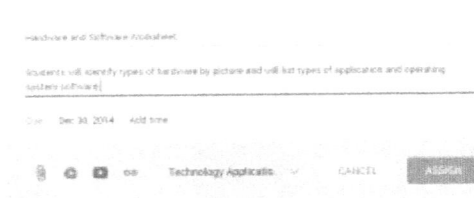

Step 3

Pick the due date (you can change it later.) After the assignment is due, the student stream will be labeled "LATE."

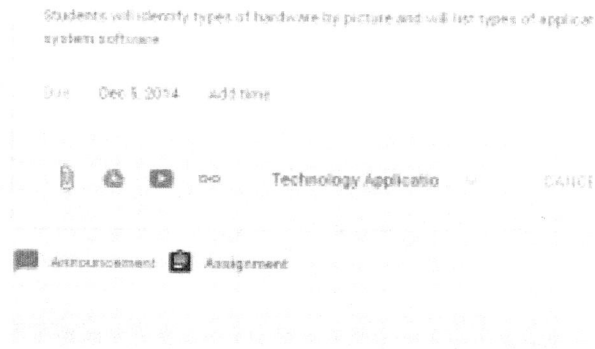

Step 4

Add an optional video/file. You can add a file to your computer, a worksheet from your Google Drive, a photo, or a connection. You should add multiple tools to your task.

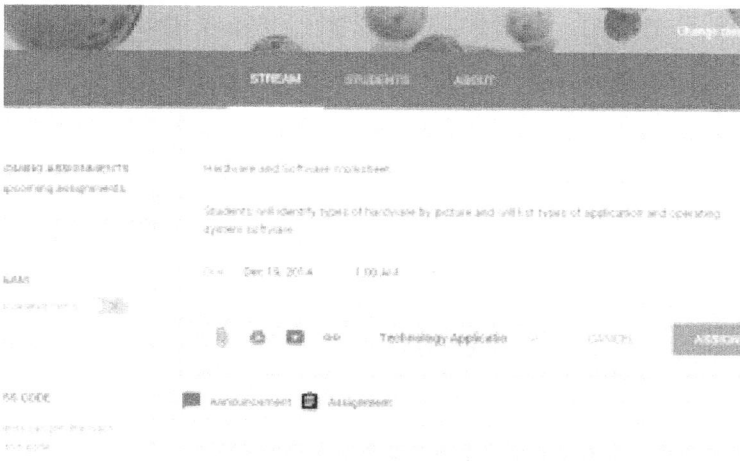

Step 5

Determine if you want students to be able to access the file, whether you want all students to write in the same document, or whether you want each one to receive a specific student name in the file name.

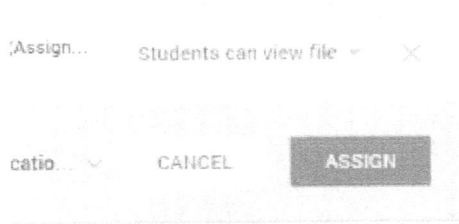

Step 6

Select the parts that you would like to delegate to.

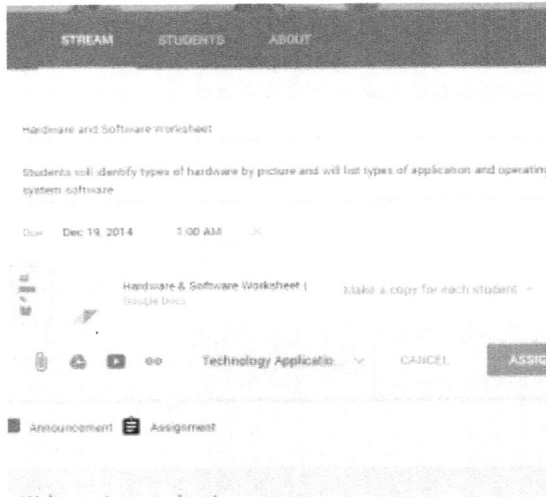

Step 7

Check that all information is right and press "ASSIGN."

Editing an Assignment

Step 1

Locate the task on your page and press three vertical dots in the top right corner, then select "Edit."

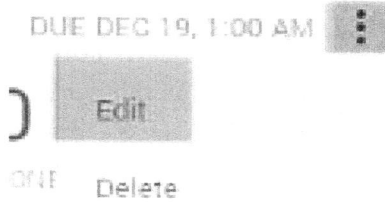

Step 2

You can change:

● Task Name

● Definition

● Due Date

● Apply additional resources

You cannot change:

● Task Worksheet

● Task Grading Worksheet

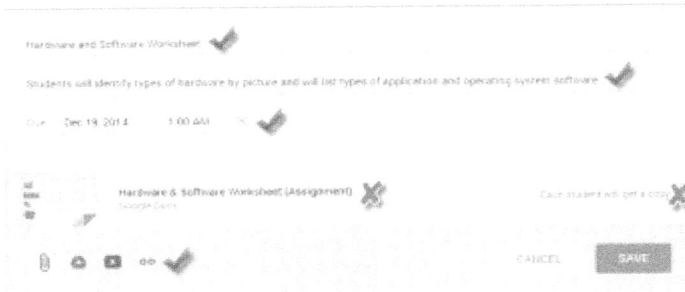

Then we have graded. Grading is a focal part of helping students understand and learn better, but it is a bit different from Google Classroom. Here, you'll learn all about how you can easily, and effectively make this grade on this platform, and how you can work within this.

To Begin with This

Now to begin, you basically need the students to turn in the work, so you should wait for students to turn in their work, and then, once it's in, it's time for you to begin. So, you log in, and you click the stream lab. Then, you can, if it isn't displayed already, check the assignments that are already there. Also, check to see who is done, and not done choose the one that's above done, and from there, you've got an expanded list on who has turned it in.

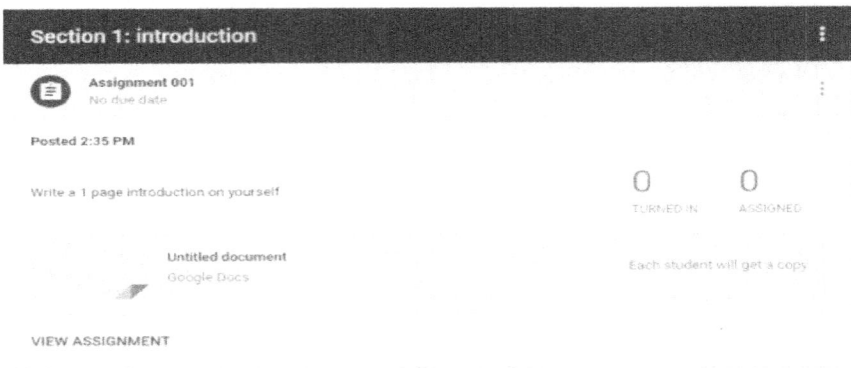

From there, you should then click on the name of the student themselves in order to see the assignment they have. From there, if they have an attachment to there, you essentially click the attachment, and then, you're given the appropriate Google app with the assignment that's on there.

At this point, you essentially will go into grading, and you can add comments and the like from there.

Commenting on Grades

At this point, you're then opening it up in the drive, and you can start to comment. If you're a teacher who likes to grade with a red pen, for example, you can easily go to the text button, change the color to red, and then comment. But it's a bit easier this time around. If you want to, you can use the feature that allows you to comment to give the appropriate feedback. To do this, you highlight what you're about to comment, choose the option to insert, and comment. At that point, type in what you need, save it, and then, it's completely uploaded in the platform. You can mark up the assignment as needed, or even leave positive comments if there is something that you should inform the student that they did well with.

At this point you can, from there, go to the classwork tab, tap the assignment name, and then view it. If you haven't changed the value of the point system yet, you can always change it. Now, choose the student file that you've finished, enter the name, and then the grade. Next, you return it to them for review.

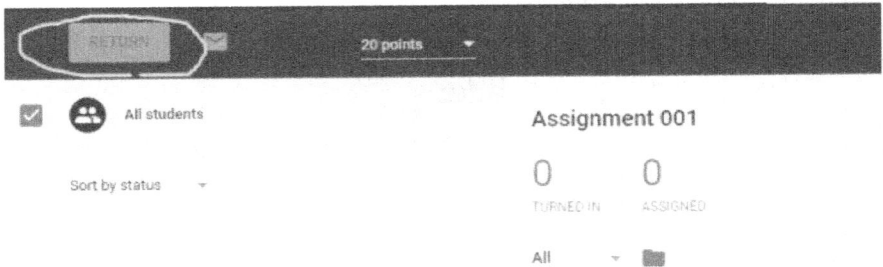

There is that instance, however, that if you want to change the grade itself, you can go to the assignment that the student has, and then enter the grade. You can also return these ungraded as needed too. Remember, that the changes to the grade only affect those not returned yet, and original ones have the same grade as before.

Returning Assignments to Students

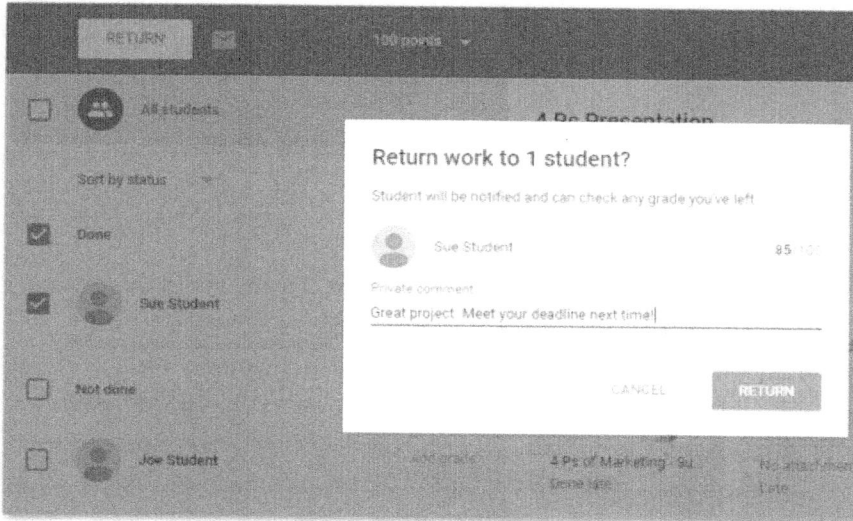

Assignments can be returned at this point to the student. You can press the box that says return assignment. Then you choose the option to return this, and it returns before it's recorded. When that happens, it will be basically done. That's up to you, and inevitably your choice. You can then press the option to return the assignment.

Now, if you have additional feedback, it'll give you an option to do that. Again, it's ultimately up to you. If you have no feedback, don't worry about this. If you do, then you should throw it in there before it's completely returned to the student. That's because the student should know. Remember, it's better to be a bit overboard with grading if you have feedback that will help students become better, and to help them understand the subject at hand.

Tips on This

The first tip that we will say is that when you're making assignments, don't use MS Word. Instead, use the Google drive apps, since they are completely integrated with the classroom system. If you do use a Microsoft word file, it'll cause the student to have to download the files once more, upload these again, and then attach them. You also need to put in the extra work with downloading and reattaching, and it's just a lot of extra fluff that you don't need. Yes, the drive files are there for a reason, and they're super easy to create. Plus, if you export a sheet from MS Word to drive, it works the same way, making it easy for everyone.

Another helpful tip is that you can actually use shortcuts to add comments onto this. You can use control alt and then M to put comments into a document on Google docs. You can then press the enter key to close the comment, and then control plus W to actually close the document itself. You can also do feedback by choosing the name of the students, and then looking at the options to see what they've submitted. You can also go to the add private comment section on this, and you can enter grades for students. You can't actually get a grade book with Google Classroom, just notify the grades though.

With Google Classroom as well, the key way to ensure that you're getting a quick feedback to students is through adding the mobile app. It allows you to add comments to various projects, and answer questions on grades.

Plus, it's integral if you want to make sure that a student. Got the assignment or not.

Another Big and important tip, is to utilize the form templates to help with grades. The form template can be used to make a sheet with the names, and a checklist of various elements, including what they're missing, homework points, and other elements. By carrying this around, you can also grade the students and it's good to have if you want to check out whether or not they have the homework done or not.

Another really cool thing is that if you want to make your grading faster, use shorthand. Google docs know what you're saying immediately, so if you use a shortcut, and you type in the letters "wc" it will automatically change this to word choice, which will communicate to the students that it's bad word choice. It makes your life so much easier, especially if you're going through grading multiple papers.

It's also important for teachers to remember that if you give an assignment back, the teacher can't edit it anymore. That means that if you have to edit anything else, they need to submit it to you again. You can notify them, and they can look at it, if they resubmit it with changes, you edit it and it's all good, you can also edit the grades by looking at it, pressing it, and then choosing the option to update the grade.

Exporting Grades

Finally, let's talk about exporting grades. Grades can be exported, and they're used to make sure that you have a place for all of them. Remember, this just displays the grades and isn't' a biodegrade, but if you want to help export these so that they're all written down, you can do this. Lots of teachers like to export these into a .csv file, or through Google sheets. You can with sheets, create an average for the class, for students, and along with this, you can actually set up arrows from a grade box to another one, which makes it faster.

To export these grades into sheets, you essentially go to Google Classroom, choose your class, and then the assignments. From here, you go to settings and choose the option to copy all of the grades into Google sheets. Then, an automatic spreadsheet is created on the drive folder, allowing you to see all the grades. Currently though, you can only export these on the desktop version of classroom, not on mobile version or via the app.

Copy all grades to Google Sheets

Download all grades as CSV

Download these grades as CSV

Now, to export these grades to a CSV file, you'll be able to have all of the grades in one place. This is good for if you're trying to keep every single grade in one place, and if you want to print these out. To do this, you essentially go to Google Classroom again, click on the class you want to choose, and then, go to settings once again, and choose an option, whether to either download the assignment grades for that one only or to download all of the assignment and question grades. For the first, you choose to download these grades as a CSV, and for the assignment and question grades, you choose to download all grades as a CSV. From there, you can find them in your downloads folder, and you can bring them up on your word processing device accordingly.

For many teachers, the element of grading is made so much easier with Google Classroom. With this, you can easily create the environment that you want to create, and from there, you've got it all set up so that students can access this easily. It's easy and simple to achieve, so you'll be able to create the best and easiest classroom experience that they can possibly have.

Chapter 8: Best Extensions and Apps that Make Google Classroom Even More Awesome + Troubleshooting Tips

Extensions and apps are usually standalone entities that make help you do more with Google Classrooms. Extensions are like plugins on the Google Chrome browser that integrates with Google Classroom. These extensions carry out special functions.

Apps are third-party applications that take advantage of Google Classrooms open API to integrate their services into the Google Classroom platform. Many apps offer added functionality like games, screen sharing, or plagiarism checks which, when integrated with Google Classroom yield powerful results.

Several other apps are from services carrying out services similar to what

Google Classroom. Instead of opening new accounts, these apps offer seamless integration. They make available your class data on their platform on Google Classroom.

Extensions

To install extensions:

1. Visit the Chrome Web store.

2. Search for the extension you want to install.

3. Click Add to Chrome to add it to your browser.

Don't forget to grant any extra permission required by the extension. Click "Add Extension" to grant these permissions.

Share to Classroom Extension

With Google Chrome, users can share content from webpages directly to Google Classrooms. This extension makes teachers easily share screens and student's work with the class. Students can share screens with teachers by clicking on the extension and clicking "Push to Teacher." Teachers can also share content with the class, which they can post as an assignment question, or as an announcement.

Insert Learning Extension

This is an extension that allows you to convert webpages to interactive class lessons. It will allow you to add sticky notes, links, videos, quizzes, and questions for discussion to the webpage and share with your students on Google Classroom. It is a great extension that will help you make your lessons more interactive and keep the students motivated.

Google Cast for Education

This is a Chrome app that lets students and tutors share screens wirelessly. With this app, teachers can control who can be added to view the screens and add students from Google Classroom.

Alice Keeler's Classroom Split

This is an extension by Alice Keeler that splits the Chrome screen and allows students to view assignment instructions and work on the assignment side by side. That way, they do not need to keep on shuttling between tabs or minimizing and maximizing constantly.

Apps

Squigl

Change showing materials into compelling discovering that keeps understudies' consideration longer.

Writable

Develop extraordinary writers with this guided work on including adjustable assignments and Google Classroom mix.

Pearson Education

This is incorporated with G-Suite™ for Education to share substance, appraisals, and lists with single sign-on get to.

ASSISTments

Offers input to instructors and understudies synchronously when understudies total assignments utilizing this free online device.

Effectively Learn

Assist understudies with building literacy abilities with writings and activities that energize comprehension and maintenance in an assortment of subjects.

Additio App

Effectively oversee everyday classroom activities, correspondence, and exercise arranging and track understudy progress with this digital grade book and classroom organizer.

Aeries

Upgrade your educational plan with this information the board, programming arrangements that permit you to make new Classroom classes, import understudy scores into Aeries, and then some.

Aeries Student Information System

Oversee and track grades, test scores, participation, and that's only the tip of the iceberg and effectively share data with understudies and guardians.

Aladdin

Improve school organization with a simple to-get to information, electronic participation records, and simple arranging and detailing instruments.

Alma

Get clear experiences into understudy execution, track participation, modify evaluating rubrics, and discuss consistently with understudies and guardians.

AristotleInsight K12

Engage understudies to become wise, safe digital citizens with this across the board classroom the executives, content separating, and detailing arrangement.

BookWidgets

Move from paper tests to intelligent tests and worksheets you can redo for your classroom, with programmed evaluating to spare you time.

BrainPOP

Draw in understudies in a wide scope of subjects with more than 1,000 educational plan adjusted enlivened films to intelligent activities and energetic games.

Troubleshooting Tips

For Teachers

To discover answers to more inquiries, visit the Google Classroom Help Community, where you can interface with different instructors.

Sign in

- I can't sign in to Classroom.

- I marked in as an understudy; however, I'm an instructor with a G-Suite for Education account.

Classes

- I can't make a class.

- How would I erase, file, or un-archive a class?

- How would I erase an understudy?

Invitations

- I can't invite understudies or educators to my group.

- I can't invite gatherings of understudies or gatherings of educators to my group.

- My understudies have issues with the class code.

Assignments

- Would i be able to reestablish an erased task?

- How would I report an issue or make a component demand?

E-mail

- I can't send or get e-mail.

- I can't invite or e-mail watchmen.

Class video gatherings

- I can't make or join a Meet gathering.

FOR STUDENT

- Inconvenience marking in.

- I marked in as an understudy and I'm an educator with a G-Suite for Education account.

I can't sign in to Classroom

- You may be attempting to sign in to Classroom with an

inappropriate record. Watch that you're utilizing the correct e-mail account. You sign in to Classroom with one of these records:

- School account—Also known as a G-Suite for Education account, this record is set up by an accredited school. It appears as though you@yourschool.edu.

- Individual Google Account—this is set up by you, or your parent or gatekeeper. Normally you utilize an individual Google Account outside of a school setting, for example, a self-teach. It appears as though you@example.com.

- G-Suite account—this is set up by your association's head. It appears as though you@yourcompany.com.

Note: You should have a functioning Internet association with sign in.

One of the reasons why you can't sign in with the correct e-mail record and a secret key possibly is because your school's principal doesn't ratify Classroom for new students. Ask your educator.

Enter Classroom

- I overlooked my secret key.

- On the off chance that your school utilizes G-Suite for Education—Ask your educator to contact the administrator to reset your secret key.

- In case you're an understudy utilizing an individual Google Account outside of a school—See change or reset your secret key.

How would I switch between client accounts?

- On the off chance that you have to sign in with an alternate client account, see Switch between accounts.

- Inconvenience marking out.

How would I sign out?

Android, Computer, iPhone and iPad

On Android, you don't sign out of a record; rather, you expel your record from your gadget. Evacuating the record doesn't erase it, so you'll, despite everything, have the option to utilize your record on different gadgets.

- In the Classroom application, tap "Menu."

- Tap Menu.

- Beside your name and e-mail, tap a down arrow and afterward manage accounts.

- Snap Manage accounts.

- Tap Google.

- (Discretionary) Tap your record.

- Tap your record.

- At the upper right, tap more and afterward remove the account.

- Tap Remove account.

- To affirm, tap Remove Account.

- Inconvenience getting to classes.

- My class code doesn't work.

In the event that your school utilizes G-Suite for Education—ask your instructor to send you another class code. In the event that the new class code doesn't work, request that your educator contact the school's administrator.

In case you're an understudy utilizing an individual Google Account outside of a school—ask your instructor to send you another class code.

A class code comprises of 6 or 7 alphanumeric characters—for instance, hjhmgrk or g5gdp1.

Note: You just utilize the class code once to select. You don't have to re-utilize the class code.

I erased or overlooked my class code

On the off chance that you erased, lost, or overlooked the class code before adding yourself to a class, ask your educator to resend the code or set another one.

Note: You just utilize the class code once to join the class. You are then taken a crack at the class and you don't have to re-utilize the code once more.

I erased my class invitation

In the event that you lose your class invitation before you added yourself to a class, ask your educator to resend the class invitation.

Note: You just utilize the class invitation once to select. You don't have to re-utilize the class invitation once more.

I unrolled from a class and need to re-enlist

In the event that you coincidentally unrolled from a class, ask your educator to resend you a class code or invitation.

Chapter 9: Google Classroom Tips Every Teacher Must Know

Great Google Classroom Tips for Teachers

Google Classroom is well known for educators across the nation and is ceaselessly being refreshed. That is the reason we chose to impart to your understudies a genuine rundown of helpful ways you can utilize the site. In this way, regardless of whether you're utilizing Classroom right now or simply investigating, read through the rundown beneath and consider how these highlights could function. Need to keep posted on new discharges and changes of highlights? Give this valuable instrument to locate a shot each month what's going on in the Classroom.

• Communicate with guardians and gatekeepers

You may welcome guardians to pursue a normal or week after week e-mail once-over on what's going on in classes for their youngsters. The messages contain pending or missed assignments for an understudy, just as updates and questions that you have gotten in the class stream.

• Help understudies remain sorted out with Google Calendar

For every exercise, Classroom consequently produces a Google Calendar and updates the schedule with future research and due dates for the understudies. Understudies will see things, for example, study days and field trips, as well. The perspective on the schedule makes it simpler to keep on target. Since new assignments or changed due dates naturally synchronize, understudies despite everything, see the most cutting-edge material.

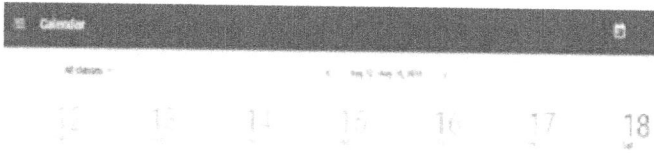

• Assign work to a subset of understudies

Instructors may designate individual understudies or a gathering of understudies inside a class to work and post declarations. This component causes instructors to isolate guidance varying, just as care group works in a coordinated effort. To discover how this functions, look at our image beneath.

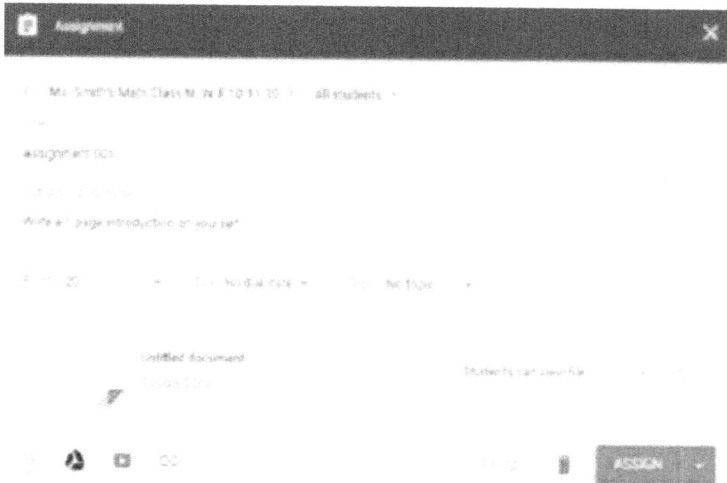

• Use comments with the Classroom portable application

Understudies and instructors can utilize the Classroom programming on cell phones running Android, iOS, and Chrome. By commenting on understudy examine in the App, you can give continuous criticism. Understudies may, likewise, comment on their assignments to pass on a thought or idea without lifting a finger.

• Explore Classroom reconciliations with different instruments

Google Classroom utilizes an API to speak with and share the entirety of your preferred assets. It joins several applications and sites, including Pear Table, Actively Know, Newsela, and many more.

Would it be a good idea for you to wish to discover more, look at our post about Google classroom-coordinated applications and sites?

• Encourage heads to utilize Classroom measurements.

In spite of the fact that this component is as yet important here for overseers — not understudies, managers may utilize the Admin reassure to show insights, for example, what number of classes were made, what number of posts were posted, and the educators are utilizing the apparatus. Access to this information will help in fitting educator support.

• Number your assignments!

Numbering your errands is perhaps the best tip that I have ever gotten. It permits you not exclusively to mastermind documents in the Classroom yet, in addition, to keep Google Drive smooth and clean.

• Use Ctrl + F to Find Numbers and Words in Classroom.

Following half a month of assignments, even the most organized Classwork page can get long. To check for watchwords or task numbers (as referenced above) on the tab, utilize the easy console route, Control + F. Show the secret to understudies, as well!

• Pick an Organizational Strategy for Using Topics.

Utilizing the themes include on the homeroom page helps facilitate understudy and educator assignments. There is a wide range of approaches to sort out yourself. There are numerous ways this can be accomplished, and what works for one instructor doesn't work for another. To instructors, this is an individual decision. Pick a method that works for your area and grade level of substance. Look at this article on How to Organize Assignments at Google Classroom for thoughts.

• Create an "Assets" Topic and Keep at the Top of the Classwork Page.

That class requires a spot to store assets, associations, rules, obviously, prospectus, etc. Mindy
Barron suggests that you fabricate a one of a kind asset and class material subject, and keep it near the top for simple access. Guarantee sure these records are just called, so understudies know what's in there.

• Create a Google Classroom Class Template.

At the point when you have chosen your favored type of sorting out for Google Classroom (and checked it!), make a duplicate of the class as your model. You can continue making a duplicate whenever you need another class and have the entirety of your themes previously created and orchestrated, and your assignments will be spared as drafts!

To cause a duplicate of a class in Google Classroom: to go to your Google

Study hall account, at that point, clicks on the class card's three dabs and

select "duplicate class." For
Increasingly far-reaching directions and tips on this idea, go to Google
Classroom's How to make a class format.

• Use Direct Links to Assignments

Knew, you may have an immediate association with a specific task? This
makes alluding understudies back to a given movement so straightforward.
Simply go to the Classwork tab, find the task, right-click on the three
specks, and duplicate the report.

• Use a Google Doc as a Syllabus

Most instructors use Google Docs to make a schedule with the goal that it
very well may be reconsidered during the year as a living book. Add
associations with outside administrations, standard assignments, basic
dates, and so on. You can likewise put to Google Classroom assignments
(see above) to keep understudies from being checked excessively long.

• Break Projects into Smaller Assignments with Separate Due Dates

Undertaking based learning is so significant, and when we keep on pushing
past the stale, one-and-done assignments, we have to contemplate how
we put this energetically in our study halls. For understudies, huge tasks
can be overwhelming, especially the individuals who haven't figured out
how to deal with their time. Giving them achievements and parting the
venture into littler assignments with checkpoints is vital.

• Create a Separate Class for Enrichment and Extension Activities

In my group, early fulfillment of your task didn't mean either extra time or
games. It has included perusing and learning programs for my students.

Consider having a different class for augmentation or improvement
programs inside Google Classroom. You may find the idea likewise and
offer advanced identifications to achieve a test or mission.

• Use Private Comments for Meaningful Feedback and Conversations with Students

One of my Google Classroom most loved highlights is the private remark application. This little instrument will help smooth out correspondence and lift the input circle with your understudies.

Instructor input is one of the primary variables for understudy advancement! Individual comments among you and your understudy are only that–own. (Nobody else will understand it.) Remember to utilize private remarks toward the finish of the errand as well as everywhere!

So this doesn't discredit the impact of eye to eye gatherings. However, it helps record with the goal that understudies can recall the criticism, just as permit understudies to associate who don't for the most part talk before the class. There are numerous spots where understudies can include private criticism.

To include a private remark from the Student Work page: Click on the task on which you need to get the contribution from the Classwork tab. Snap-on the "View Task" button. Select the understudy from the left-hand list. You can see "Include Private Comment" at the base of the right-hand section. Snap to type in and present your understudy's private remark. You can now also include private remarks from inside the understudy's archive utilizing the most recent reviewing highlight in Google Classroom.

Snap the task. You might want to give criticism from the Classwork tab. Snap the "View Task" tab. Snap the understudy record you need to give a contribution on. To make a private message, utilize the board at the top.

• Use Private Comments for Reflection

A few instructors take the private remarks highlight above and beyond and make it part of the task by necessitating that understudies include a reflection as a private remark after they present their activities. Sean Fahey recommends utilizing an open:

Finished inquiry or gives understudies a brief like, "What did you like most about the task?" or "What part tested you the most?"

• Attach a Template Document for Each Assignment

You can see the task page in Google Classroom, and see a thumbnail for every understudy. That permits you to see change initially or the absence of it. Regardless of whether you don't have a format for your undertaking that you include a spared dark report as a kind of perspective so you can present get a brief look at the thumbnails!

• Invite Teachers that are Hesitant to Use Google Classroom to Be a Student or Co-Teacher in Your Class

From the outset, I suggest inviting them as a visitor, so they get a comprehension of how this functions before they can join and alter the class as a co-educator. Inside a class, co-instructors can do anything you need. They are welcoming understudies.

Click on the welcome instructor's symbol to invite you as a co-educator and type in your name or e-mail address and press "Invite." Click on the "Invite Students" symbol to welcome an educator as an understudy and type in their name or e-mail address and afterward press welcome.

Chapter 10: What's New in the Google Classroom

1. The drag and Drop On The Classwork Page

This is a sort of new Classwork page where educators can remain made with chart their classes. In any case, we comprehend that teachers sort out their classes explicitly propensities and need extra adaptability in their classroom tools. So now, you can relocate whole topics and individual Classwork things, altering them effectively on the page. You can drag a whole point to a particular zone on the Classwork page, or drag singular things inside—and in—topics. This accommodation pushed a year earlier on versatile, and now it's the ideal open entryway for it to hit the web.

2. The invigorated Us

Directly from now, you'll persistently observe that Classroom has a superior look and sentiments, first on the page, and soon in the Classroom versatile applications. Over the most recent couple of years, we recognizable Google's new material subject with having more consistency across Google things and platforms. Among the changes, you'll see an unyieldingly normal game plan stream—despite another way to deal with overseeing shape, covering, iconography, and typography, on both the web and the advantageous application. We're besides making the class code less hard to access and experience so students can without a truly amazing stretch find and join. At long last, we're giving 78 new topics custom portrayals, going from history to math to hairdressing to photography. Eventually, you can re-attempt your Classroom like never before as of now.

3. Refreshed Training and Backing

At last, with its new tools and progressively, different changes come essentially for much better help. In the Teacher Social order, you'll find resuscitated records in our First Day of Classroom training with the new course of action and highlights we turned out in 2018. While we're pounding perpetually, we assembled a predominant than whenever in late memory Help Center, got along with our District and thing gathering.

The following are past changes to Google Classroom:

Other/Past Changes to Google Classroom Before 2019-2020 School Year

1. Post Questions

Phan clarifies, "You can present inquiries on your group and permit students to have conversations by reacting to one another's answers (or not, contingent upon the setting you pick.) For instance, you could post a video and pose students to answer an inquiry about it, or post an article and request that they compose a passage accordingly."

2. Reuse Assignments

In the event that you reuse educational programs quite a long time after year-or if nothing else reuse archives, there is an update you may like. Phan clarifies, "Presently you can reuse assignments, declarations or inquiries from any of your classes — or any class you co-educate, regardless of whether it's from a year ago or a week ago. When you pick what you'd prefer to duplicate, you'll likewise have the option to make changes before you post or dole out it."

3. Improved Calendar Reconciliation

We love changes that improve the work procedure. "In the next month, Classroom will, therefore, make a calendar for all of your classes in Google Calendar. All assignments with a due date will be normally added to your gathering calendar and kept awake with the most recent. You'll have the choice to see your calendar from inside Classroom or on Google Calendar, where you can truly incorporate class events like field trips or guest speakers."

4. Knock a post

Staying posts on sites, tweets, or Facebook refreshes has, for quite some time, been a thing. Presently you can do it on Google Classroom too by moving any post to the top.

5. Due dates discretionary

Undertaking based learning, Self-coordinated learning? Creator ed? On the off chance that you utilize long haul ventures or other due-date-less assignments, you would now be able to make assignments without due dates in Google Classroom.

6. Connect a Google Form to a post

In case you're an aficionado of Google Forms (here's a post about utilizing Google Forms to make a self-evaluated test), this is a chance you'll appreciate it. Phan clarifies, "Numerous teachers have been utilizing Google Forms as a simple method to relegate a test, test, or study to the class. Coming in the following barely any weeks, teachers and students will before long have the option to append Google Forms from Drive to posts and assignments, and get a connection in Classroom to handily see the appropriate responses."

7. YouTube Usefulness

Love YouTube, yet stressed over stunning content? Google hears you.

"Since it in like manner contains content that an organization or school presumably won't consider commendable, a month prior, we moved advanced YouTube settings for all Google Applications spaces as an Additional Help. These settings empower Applications overseers to keep the YouTube chronicles detectable for set apart in users, similarly as set apart out users on frameworks supervised by the manager.

Ways to Utilize Google Classroom

At the point when a task, exercise, or unit doesn't work, include your own remarks or have students include their own input), at that point, label it or save it to an alternate folder for correction.

- Adjust the educational program to different teachers.

- Offer information with a professional learning network.

- Keep tests of model composition for arranging.

- Label your educational program.

- Request day by day, week after week, by-semester, or yearly criticism from students and guardians utilizing Google Forms.

- Offer unknown composing tests with students.

- See what your assignments resemble from the students' perspective.

- Flip your classroom. The tools to distribute recordings and offer assignments are centered on Google Applications for Training.

- Impart task standards with students.

- Let students pose inquiries secretly.

- Let students make their own computerized arrangement of their preferred work.

- Make a rundown of endorsed inquire about sources. You can likewise separate this by student, gathering, understanding level, and that's just the beginning.

- Post a declaration for students, or students and guardians.

- Plan progressively versatile learning encounters for your students— in higher ed, for instance.

- Have students outline their own development after some time utilizing Google Sheets.

- Offer due dates with coaches outside the classroom with an open calendar.

- E-mail students separately, or as gatherings. Even better, watch as they speak with each other.

- Make tests that grade itself utilizing Google Forms.

- Control file rights (see, alter, duplicate, download) on a file-by-file premise.

- Have student's clergyman venture-based learning antiquities.

- As a teacher, you can work together with different teachers (same evaluation by group, same content across grade level.)

- Support advanced citizenship by means of a shared connection that is recorded.

- Use Google Calendar for due dates, occasions outside the classroom, and other significant 'sequential information.'

- Discuss carefully with students who might be reluctant to 'talk' with you face to face.

- Smooth out cross-curricular tasks with different teachers.

- Total and distribute normally got to sites to ensure everybody has the same access, same archives, same connections, and same information.

- Vertically-adjust students are learning by creating and sharing "milestone" student assignments that reflect the dominance of explicit measures.

- Empower a typical language by unloading principles and offer area-wide.

- Urge students to utilize their cell phones for formal learning. By getting to archives, YouTube channels, bunch correspondence, advanced portfolio pieces, and more on a BYOD gadget, students will get an opportunity to consider them to be as some different option from an only for-diversion gadget.

- Make and distribute 'power gauges' (with students, different teachers, and different schools) for straightforwardness and coordinated effort.

- Elevate distributed as well as school-to-class communications students with different students, students with different teachers, and teachers with different teachers.

- Make 'by-need' bunches as classes–dependent on understanding level, for instance.

- Check which students have gotten to which assignments.

- Give the student input.

- Add voice remarks to student composing (this requires an outsider application to do as such.)

- Assist students with making content-explicit YouTube channels.

- 'Shut circuit distribute' commented on exploring papers as indicated by explicit styles (MLA, APA, and so on.) or other something else 'confounding' work.

- Make an advanced parking garage for questions.

- Control computerized leave slips.

- Rather than schoolwork, dole out willful 'exercise extensions' for students. At the point when questions emerge about authority or evaluations, allude to who got to and finished what, when.

- Make folders of incidental exercise materials—advanced adaptations of writings, and so forth.

- Appreciate more brilliant conferencing with students and guardians with simple to-get to work, information, composing, input, get to information, etc.

- Save pdf's or different depictions of advanced assets, in general, got to folders.

- Make an information divider, however, with spreadsheets and shading coding.

- Make sub-work or make-up work simple to get to.

- Gather information. This can occur in an assortment of ways, from utilizing Google Forms, extraction to Google Sheets, or your own in-house strategy.

- Give brief critical for learning.

- See who's finished what–and when initially.

- Track when students turn-in work.

- Since getting to be followed, search for designs in student propensities those that get to assignments quickly, those that reliably come back to work, etc. And impart those patterns (namelessly) to students as a method of conveying "best practices in learning" for students who may not in any case think

- Particularly guidance, through tiering, gathering, or Sprout's spiraling.

- Make bunches dependent on preparation, enthusiasm, understanding level, or different variables for instructing and learning.

- Use Google Forms to survey students, make per user intrigue reviews, and that's only the tip of the iceberg.

- Model a work referred to the page.

- Make reference sheets.

- Structure computerized group building exercises.

- Make a paperless classroom.

- Offer all-inclusive and as often as possible got to assignments– venture rules, year-long due dates, math formulas, content-regional realities, recorded courses of events, and so forth.

Chapter 11: FAQs about Google Classroom

As a teacher, there are a lot of different options that you can use to make the most out of your classroom, and you may be curious as to why Google Classroom is the best option to help you out. There are many questions that you may have that pertain to Google Classroom. Some of the questions that you may have about Google Classroom include:

How Do I Create Google Classroom More Interactive And Engaging For My Pupils?

To create learning content more lively for Pupils, look at mixing the kinds of tools you share in Google Classroom together. Along with G-Suite tools such as Google Slides and Google Docs, students and teachers may share different kinds of media, such as pictures, links to screencast videos, and sites. Some educators give many different choices to pupils for submitting their job. By way of instance, you may offer students the decision to answer a reading assignment withdrawing, a movie clip, or a remark which shows their belief.

If you are looking to create an interactive hub for pupils, you could look at doing so on the Stream page of Google Classroom. The Stream is a feed-in in which everybody in the course can find upcoming assignments and statements, and it is the very first thing. A blogger that writes about Google Classroom Alice Keeler proposes using Screencastify to Post messages and recommends utilizing the Stream to post your course agenda.

Some educators use class discussion to be installed by the Stream Boards, where pupils can socialize on the internet by asking questions or commenting on the posts of each other. These discussion boards will help improve class participation and extend pupils more equity in getting their voices heard (or read) from the course. With talks, you may use the Stream as a closed social network of types. Also, it can be a fantastic way to help children practice employing all sorts of different electronic citizenship abilities in a "walled garden" kind of setting.

What Other Programs And Sites Incorporate With Google Classroom?

There are sites and countless external programs that incorporate with Google Classroom. A number of those apps may associate with Google, but others release and make their own third party. Integrating EdTech tools may be a means if you are using Google Classroom widely. By way of instance, say you would like your pupils to examine some vocabulary words utilizing Quizlet; you may use the Google Classroom integration assigned and to talk about a flashcard. Or, if you're on the lookout for learning content on the internet, you can find instructional Posts, amongst others— you'll get all types of Posts, videos Khan Academy, and BrainPop, and integrations with publishers such as Newsela.

Our Post Sites and Nine Apps, which are contained in the record, do not end there, although Google Classroom covers a few of them. Odds are there is a way to connect it when there's a program or site you enjoy with your students.

Where Do I Find More Thoughts About Using Google Classroom?

In case you're looking for Information Regarding Google Classroom, check out Google to get merchandise upgrades for Education's Twitter feed, ideas for teachers, and a newsletter about G-Suite for Instruction Solutions. Lovers of Google Classroom are blogging, tweeting, and podcasting about all the ways. With countless EdTech pros and educators innovating with Google Classroom, experimenting, and field-testing, it's simple to discover inspiration and hints online.

Do not be afraid to get as you are using Google Classroom Creative with hacks your strategies, and advanced uses for the stage. Like tools, Google Classroom is the way it functions will look different from classroom to classroom and exactly what you make of this. What is most important is to discover tools and the strategies within Google Classroom, which work best for your pupils and you. You're able to talk about the ways you are using Google Classroom together with your students now by leaving a Teacher Inspection.

What Reproduces into The Stream Webpage?

Things that copy:

- The course name

- The section

- The topic

- The room amount

- The course code

- Posts and opinions

What Reproduces into The Classwork Webpage?

Classwork, copies, drafts, are missions for the new class. In case you have permission, you can use an attachment copy.

Things that replicate:

- Topics

- Assignments, quiz assignments, questions, and their attachments

- Rubrics added to duties

- Materials and their attachments

- Documents or attachments that you do not have permission to replicate

What Copies into The Grades Page?

Until you include in the category, the Grades page is blank Pupils and post classwork, like a query or an assignment.

Things that are repeated:

- Classwork Posts, like questions or assignments.

- Your grading method.

- Your grade classes.

- Pupils and their ranges.

What Reproduces to the People Page?

Individuals that move:

- The Principal instructor.

- Co-teachers.

- Pupils.

What Reproduces into The Settings Page?

Settings which replicate:

- All of the Class details, except the room number.

- All Grading configurations, including your regular calculation preferences and your grade classes.

- The settings: They come back to their default settings.

- The course code: A code that is brand new is made for the category.

What's A College Account?

A college account is an accredited school. Your college's admin manages and generates these records. The accounts appear like you@yourschool.edu.

How Do I Begin with a College Account?

Your college's if you are a teacher or pupil in a college "Admin password" and provides your e-mail.

Note: Should you use Classroom at a college and need to get Classroom use your college account to register in.

What's A Private Google Account?

A Google Account is an account that you produce. You are very likely to utilize a Google Account that is private with a Classroom such as a homeschool or a facility. The accounts appear like you@example.com.

How Do I Begin with a Private Account?

Users make their own Google Accounts. For more information, see "Create a Google Account."

Kids who do not fulfill the age requirements to create a Google Account that is private may be in a position to have an account created by a grownup. To learn more, see "Create a Google Account for a child."

Notice: Every Nation has its minimum age requirement for producing a Google Account. See "Age demands."

Can users with private Google Accounts have access to exactly the very same attributes as other reports?

No. Having a Google Account:

- Kids that have an account teach or cannot take courses.

- Classmates can't be e-mailed by Pupils.

- Teachers cannot invite guardians to register for summaries.

What are A G-Bundle Accounts?

There is A G-Bundle account Utilized in Massive organizations that operate among the subsequent G-Bundle variations:

- G-Bundle Fundamental

- G-Suite Business

- G-Suite Enterprise

- G-Suite for Nonprofits

- The accounts appear like you@yourcompany.com

Is it easy to get started with Google Classroom?

Yes, it is really easy to work with Google Classroom, but you do need to remember that it is necessary to have the Google Apps for Education, and your domain needs to be verified. We explained how to do this a little bit how to get the Google Apps for Education as well as setting up your domain so make sure that you follow these instructions so that the application can be reviewed right from the beginning.

How are the Apps for Education and Classroom connected?

To keep things simple, Google Classroom is not able to work without the help of Google Apps for Education. While you are able to use the Apps for Education all on its own, you will find that using Google Classroom is going to help to make all of it organized, and it is much easier to work with. With the help of both the Classroom and Apps working together, both the students and the teachers are able to access the spreadsheets, slideshows, and documents as well as other links without having to worry about attachments and more. Even giving and receiving assignments and grades are easier when these two are combined together.

In addition, there is the option to download the Classroom Mobile app, which will make it easier to access your classes whenever and wherever you would like. This is going to be great for students who are on the go and don't have time to always look through their laptop to see announcements. Even teachers are able to use this mobile app to help them get up assignments and announcements when they are on the go so they can concentrate on other thanks later on.

Does it cost to use Google Classroom?

One of the best things about using Google Classroom is that it is completely free. All you need is a bit of time to help get it all set up, but it will not include any out of pocket costs to make it work. You will have to wait about two weeks in the beginning for your application to be reviewed before you are able to use the class, so consider setting this up early to prevent issues with falling behind.

You will never have to pay for anything when you are using Google Classroom. If you run into a vendor who is asking for you to pay for Google Classroom, you should report them to Google. It is highly likely that this is a fake vendor, so do not work with them or provide them with any of your payment information. Google Classroom is, and always will be, free for you to use.

Can I still use Classroom if it is disabled on my domain?

One of the nice things about working with Classroom is that even if it has been disabled on a certain domain, you are still able to use it. With that being said, there are going to be a few restrictions. While you may still be able to get access to a lot of the features, such as Google Drive, Google Docs, and Gmail, you may not be able to see some of the slides, docs, and sheets that were saved in the classroom. It is always best to have your domain turned on when you are working in Google Classroom because this ensures that you are able to use all of the features that are available through it.

Do I need to have Gmail enabled to use classroom?

It is not necessary to have Gmail enabled in order to use the Google Classroom. You are able to use the Classroom as much as you would like without enabling Gmail, but you would find that you wouldn't be able to receive notifications if the Gmail account isn't turned on. If you would like to have some notifications sent to you, you need to have Gmail enabled.

If you are not that fond of using the Gmail account for this, it is possible to set up your own e-mail server to make it work. This way, you will still be able to receive the notifications that are needed from the Classroom while using the e-mail server that you like the most.

Will I have to work with ads on Google Classroom?

Many people like to work with Google Classroom because they don't have to worry about seeing ads all over the place. This was designed for educational purposes, and Google recognizes that people don't want to have to fight with ads all of the time when they are learning. You can rest assured that Google and Classroom are not going to take your information and use it for advertising. This is part of the privacy and security that is offered with Google Classroom, which will protect both the student and the teacher from any phishing or spam.

Chapter 12: Smarter Ways to Utilize Google Classroom

As soon as an assignment, lesson, or unit does not function, add your personal remarks — or have students put in their own comments), then label it or store it to another folder for revision.

- Align curriculum with other educators.

- Share information with the learning community.

- Keep samples of exemplar.

- Tag your program.

- Ask for daily by-semester or feedback from parents and pupils.

- Share anonymous writing samples with pupils.

- See what your homework looks like from the pupils' point-of-view.

- Flip your own classroom. The resources to print videos and discuss missions are at the center of Google Apps for Education.

- Communicate assignment standards.

- Let pupils ask questions individually.

- Let students make their own portfolios of their work that preferred.

- Make a list of research resources that accepted. You might distinguish that by reading level, group, student, and much more.

- Post for parents and students, or a statement for students.

- Design learning experiences for the students—for instance, in higher education.

- Students graph their development over time.

- Share due dates together with mentors beyond the classroom using a general calendar.

- E-mail learners individually or as groups. Watch because they communicate together.

- Produce a test that results in itself using Google Forms.

- Control file rights (see, edit, duplicate, download) onto a file-by-file basis.

- Have students curate project-based studying artifacts.

- As a teacher, you also can collaborate with other educators (same tier by group, same material across grade level.)

- Invite digital citizenship through peer-reviewed interaction that documented.

- Use Google calendar for due dates, events away from the classroom, along with another significant 'chronological arrangement.'

- Communicate digitally with pupils who might be reluctant to 'speak' with you in person.

- Streamline jobs.

- Aggregate and print accessed sites to be sure everybody has the same accessibility, same files, same connections, and same details.

- Vertically-align the pupil to learn from curating and sharing "milestone" student missions that reflect mastery of criteria.

- Invite a frequent speech by unpacking standards and discuss district-wide.

- Invite students to use their telephones. By obtaining files, YouTube stations, set communication, electronic portfolio pieces, and much more on a BYOD apparatus, pupils will have an opportunity to view their telephone as something apart from a for-entertainment device.

- Make and print 'power criteria' (together with students, other educators, and other colleges) for transparency and cooperation.

- Promote peer or school-to-school connections—students with different students, students with different educators, and teachers with different teachers.

- Produce 'by-need' classes as courses—according to reading level, for instance.

- Assess which pupils have obtained which duties.

- Supply opinions to students.

- Add voice remarks to student writing (that needs a third-party program to do this.)

- Aid students generate content-specific YouTube stations.

- 'Closed-circuit print' annotated research papers based on certain styles (MLA, APA, etc.) or other differently 'perplexing' work.

- Share demonstrations.

- Produce an electronic parking lot'' for queries.

- Administer digital departure slips.

- For pupils, assign voluntary' lesson extensions' rather than homework. Consult with who obtained and finished exactly what, and when questions arise about grades or predominate.

- Create folders of lesson Matters—digital versions of texts, etc.

- Appreciate smarter conferencing with parents and students with work, information, composing, opinions, access information that is easy-to-access, etc.

- Save snapshots of resources in folders or PDFs.

- Produce a data wall with color-coding and spreadsheets.

- Make make-up work or sub-work.

- Collect information. This can occur by using extraction into Google Sheets Google Forms, or even your very own procedure.

- Give feedback.

- See if —who finished what.

- When pupils turn-in track, work.

- Since accessibility is monitored, start looking for patterns in pupil customs — people who get assignments instantly, those who always return to work, etc. — and communicate these tendencies (anonymously) to pupils as a means of communicating "best practices in learning" for students who may not otherwise believe.

- Differentiate education through bloom, group, or tier.

- Create classes or alternative variables for studying and teaching.

- Use Google Forms to survey pupils, create much more, and reader interest polls.

- Model a work cited page.

- Refer to sheets.

- Design pursuits that are electronic.

- Produce a classroom.

- Share universal and often accessed missions — job guidelines, yearlong because dates, math formulas, content-area details, historical timelines, etc.

Strategies for Getting Started with Google Classroom

Combine the Google Classroom revolution! It is going to fully alter how you communicate and socialize, supply homework on your course, and supply your pupil's abilities!

Google Classroom is a program help educators and pupils communicate, organize, collaborate, and handle duties, go awry, and more! Google designed this program for educators and pupils, and they would like it to be your mission supervisor for Google Drive and outside.

Google Classroom is an easy-to-use program. However, there are a whole lot of methods you will learn the way on. I have assembled a few of the suggestions I have learned while using Google Classroom to this infographic that is convenient. Establish your classroom for success and prepare yourself to be amazed at the simplicity and ease Google Classroom brings to an own workflow

Use Google Chrome

To familiarise with the attributes in Google Classroom, the Google Chrome browser should be used by students. Google Chrome is a learning environment for many things from Google.

Listed below are just three extensions that make GC better.

Create Naming Conventions for Your Classes

Produce a descriptive and constant naming convention for your courses before beginning incorporating them. Think about such as the term or school year. Case in point: 7th Stage U.S. Background 17-18.

Create Naming Conventions for Your Assignments

Consistency in naming your homework can aid you, and your pupils find what you want. Consider numbering your homework and be more descriptive. Make sure you incorporate the learning aim! This may help you find documents. Instance: 035 Poe writer Study.

Use Topics to Organize

- Create topics to arrange tools, assignments, and your content.

- On the Classwork webpage, click "Create" to include new themes.

- I propose developing a subject for yearlong resources, so they are simple to find, such as "Class Resources."

- Contemplate what subjects match your program the ideal. Here are some suggestions:

- Teachers look at coordinating by topic area.

- Secondary teachers, look at coordinating by mission kind like daily work, projects, assignments, labs, studying, etc.

Differentiate Assignments

Use one which allows you to give homework. Every student does not need to perform the same mission.

Get the Mobile App

Get the program that is a cell for your pupils to get Google Classroom and you anytime, anyplace. Bonus! The program will send push alarms to let pupils know when they have a new mission - Accessible to Android and iOS.

Conclusion

Thank you for making it to the end. Google Classroom now a day has been used properly for homework communication, school management, and student communication; however, the general use is limited to these properties, while Google Classroom has a lot to do beyond these simple basic functions. This is an interesting remark that is a free and cost-free tool, which is a significant feeling when used in most sectors of Pakistani education. This is Google's first year in the classroom, and recognizing a platform over time is becoming a major hurdle for students and teachers. An important conclusion from this research is that teachers cannot understand the Google Classroom interface. If the administrator can minimize usability and simplify with some additional features, such as video resources, you can radically improve the efficiency of Google Classroom.

Where can I find more ideas on using Google Classroom?

If you're looking for original information in the Google Classroom, check out Google Education's Twitter section for updated articles, teacher ideas, videos, and much more in the G-Suite for Education section. Many Google Classroom fans create tweets, blogs, and even podcasts in all the ways students use the platform. For many technology teachers and professionals who do field tests and further develop with Google Classroom, the suggestions and incentives of all online teachers are simple to find.

When using Google Classroom, do not be afraid to be creative with your methods, hacking, and creative use of the platform. Like most EdTech devices, you think Google Classroom is and how it works will be really unique between classes. The important thing is to learn the methods and tools of Google Classroom that are best for you and your students. By sharing teacher comments, you can share with students how to use Google Classroom.

The concept of education has recently changed from teacher to student. Previously, teachers took on the role of an information society, but their work has now expanded. There is a strong emphasis on integrating technology/innovation in the classroom with intelligent teaching methods that focus on empowering students to achieve their chosen learning goals (Hwang, Wang and Lai, 2015.) Technology encourages greater student involvement (Northey, Bucic, Govind and Chylinski, 2015,) which is very important for achieving the desired learning objectives (Bolkan, 2015.)

Education is often confused with the school environment to understand how to be personal and independent of students (Graham, 2006.) Educational technology promoters and experts have found hybrid educational centers (Hinkelman, 2018.) The terms mixed learning, mixed learning, and mixed learning are used (Breslow and Zhao, 2013.) Mixed learning allows students and teachers to make regular progress after changing the policy presentation. It should be noted that the goal is not just to integrate technology into the classroom; moreover, educational objectives should define other teaching methods (Kristine and O'Byrne, 2015.)

Now teachers can use different educational technologies in combination with traditional classroom environments to improve student learning conditions. In 2014, Google Education (GAFE) introduced the Google Classroom program. Students and teachers can use this program and make it perfect for developing countries with limited funding. This can serve as a framework for knowledge management in schools, colleges, and universities. Teachers can successfully pass the time using Google Classroom.

Made in the USA
Monee, IL
12 August 2020